POTPOURRI

Text by Gail Duff
Illustrations by Charlotte Wess

CRESCENT BOOKS

Editorial Direction: Joanna Lorenz
Art Direction: Bobbie Colgate-Stone
Production Control: Susan Brown
Hand Lettering: Leonard Currie

First published in 1990 by Pyramid Books,
an imprint of the Octopus Publishing Group,
Michelin House, 81 Fulham Road, London SW3 6RB.

This 1990 edition published by Crescent Books,
distributed by Outlet Book Company, Inc.,
a Random House Company,
225 Park Avenue South, New York,
New York 10003.

Printed and bound in Spain

ISBN 0–517–03082–9

87654321

CONTENTS

$\mathcal{I}$NTRODUCTION

MAKING POT POURRI is a great pleasure, and the end result
will continue to delight for many months after. Pot pourri
keeps the scents of summer in your house throughout the
winter and, when a gift, it is a constant reminder of the
giver. Pots pourris have the ability to calm, relax, and
enliven, and working with the deliciously scented
ingredients is therapeutic as well as highly enjoyable.
From the sixteenth century to the beginning of the
twentieth, the making of pot pourri and other fragrant

preparations was an art known to nearly every country housewife. Recipes varied from simple mixtures of dried flowers produced from the smallest cottage gardens to the complicated and often expensive creations made in the country house still-room.

There are really two methods of making pot pourri, a dry and a moist. The easiest, the dry pot pourri, is made by simply mixing dry ingredients and then leaving them to mature for six weeks in a sealed polythene or polyethyl bag before use. A finished pot pourri is most often kept in an open bowl. Most of the recipes in this book are for dry pots pourris – use dry ingredients unless fresh are specified, and store in plastic bags for six weeks before using.

For a moist pot pourri, the main flower ingredient, usually rose petals, must be half dried first before being layered with salt and sometimes spices, and left under a weight to ferment. Any liquid that collects after a few weeks is poured off, and the mixture is left until it is a dry cake.

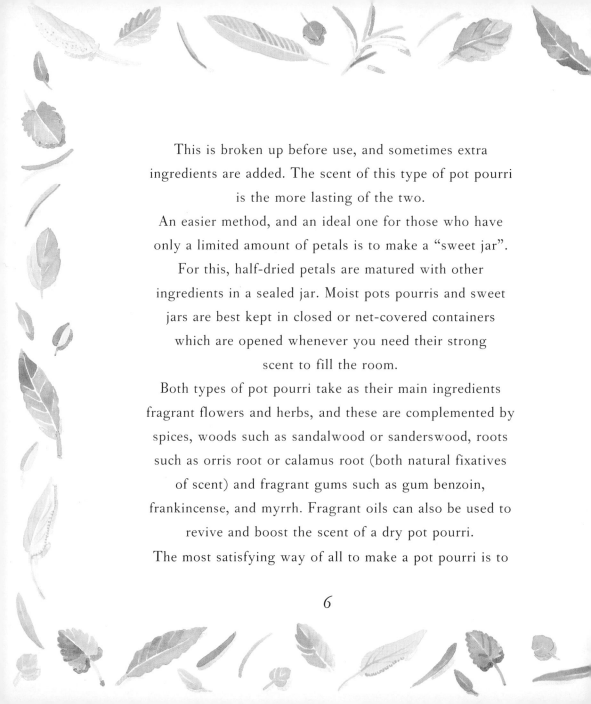

This is broken up before use, and sometimes extra
ingredients are added. The scent of this type of pot pourri
is the more lasting of the two.

An easier method, and an ideal one for those who have
only a limited amount of petals is to make a "sweet jar".
For this, half-dried petals are matured with other
ingredients in a sealed jar. Moist pots pourris and sweet
jars are best kept in closed or net-covered containers
which are opened whenever you need their strong
scent to fill the room.

Both types of pot pourri take as their main ingredients
fragrant flowers and herbs, and these are complemented by
spices, woods such as sandalwood or sanderswood, roots
such as orris root or calamus root (both natural fixatives
of scent) and fragrant gums such as gum benzoin,
frankincense, and myrrh. Fragrant oils can also be used to
revive and boost the scent of a dry pot pourri.

The most satisfying way of all to make a pot pourri is to

grow and dry many of the flowers and herbs yourself. Flower heads and petals are best dried on wooden frames covered with muslin. Herbs can be hung up in bunches in a dry, airy room. For a dry pot pourri, all the ingredients must be dried until they are crisp. For the moist type or for the sweet jar they should only be half dried, until they feel dry on the surface but are still flexible like leather. If you do not have a garden, you can still make a dry pot pourri by buying all the ingredients. Herbs and spices can be bought in most supermarkets. Flower and herb oils can be bought from herbalists.

If you do not have a particular ingredient stated in the recipe, do not despair. Pot pourri recipes are very flexible. Give your mixture a sniff. Is it pleasant without the missing ingredient? Can you think of anything else that would complement the other scents just as well? If you can, you are well on the way to creating your own first pot pourri recipe.

PERFUMED SWEET PINK PETALS

A pot pourri with a delicate appearance and a sweet, gently spiced fragrance.

Mix together 2 cups rosebuds, 1 cup rose petals, ½ cup hibiscus flowers, ½ cup each paeony petals and poppy petals, 4 tablespoons dried orange peel, crushed, 4 tonquin (tonka) beans, grated or crushed, 2 vanilla pods, chopped and crushed, 2 tablespoons bayberry powder and 4 tablespoons orris root powder. Add 2 drops rose oil and 3 drops French musk oil, and mix well.

8

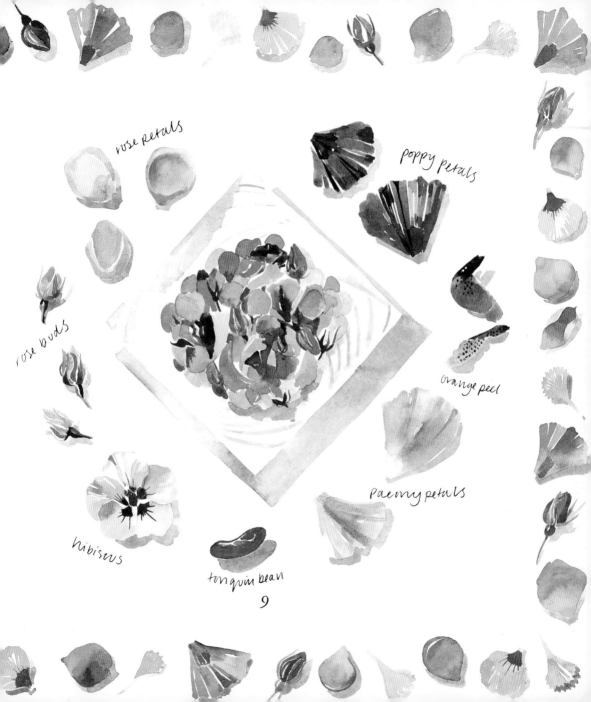

rose petals

poppy petals

orange peel

rose buds

Paeony petals

hibiscus

tonquin bean

9

A Bowl of
Herbs & Roses

*Mixing herbs and rose petals gives a fresh, clean
everyday scent that makes a pot pourri suitable for
any living area or kitchen.*

*Mix together 2 cups rose petals, 1 cup lavender
flowers, 4 tablespoons each southernwood,
rosemary, thyme, marjoram, hyssop, and crushed
bay leaves. Crush and add 2 cinnamon sticks and
2 tablespoons juniper berries. Put in 3 tablespoons
orris root powder, 2 drops each rose, lavender and
rosemary oil, and mix well.*

rosemary

cinnamon
sticks

thyme

rose petals

marjoram

bay
leaf

lavender

southernwood

hyssop

juniper berries

11

ROSE GARDEN POT POURRI

This traditional rose pot pourri has a sweet, delicate scent that is suitable for the living room or bedroom.

Mix together 3 cups rose petals, 1/2 cup lemon verbena, 4 tablespoons lavender flowers, 4 tablespoons marjoram, and 1 tablespoon crushed dried orange peel. Crumble in 4 cinnamon sticks and grate in 1/2 nutmeg. Add 2 tablespoons orris root powder and mix well. Add 6 drops rose oil and 3 drops lemon verbena oil and mix again.

rose petals

lemon
verbena

cinnamon
sticks

marjoram

nutmeg

orange peel

lavender

13

MEDLEY OF GARDEN HERBS

This has a fresh, savoury scent and is best in the hallway, dining room, or kitchen.

Mix together 2 cups lemon verbena, 1 cup lemon balm, ¹/₂ cup each rosemary, lavender, thyme, sage and crushed bay leaves, plus any dried blue or yellow flowers to add colour. Crush and add 2 cinnamon sticks, 4 tablespoons lovage root and 4 tablespoons dried lemon peel. Put in 4 tablespoons orris root powder, 4 drops lavender oil, and 2 drops each rosemary and lemon verbena oil.

bay leaf

lemun verbena

yellow flowers

lavender

thyme

lemon balm

sage

lemun peel

cinnamon sticks

rosemary

15

A SWEET JAR
OF ROSES

*A simple moist sweet jar, made with only rose
petals and sweet spices. It has a strong,
warm scent.
Mix 3 cups half-dried rose petals with ¹/₂ cup fine,
pure sea salt, 4 tablespoons orris root powder, 1
tablespoon ground cinnamon, ¹/₂ tablespoon ground
nutmeg, and 2 tablespoons sieved muscovado
sugar. Put the mixture into a jar and push in 1
whole vanilla pod. Seal the jar tightly and leave
the pot pourri for 3 weeks. Shake the jar well, and
remove the vanilla pod before putting the pot pourri
into its final container.*

rose petals

cinnamon   nutmeg

17

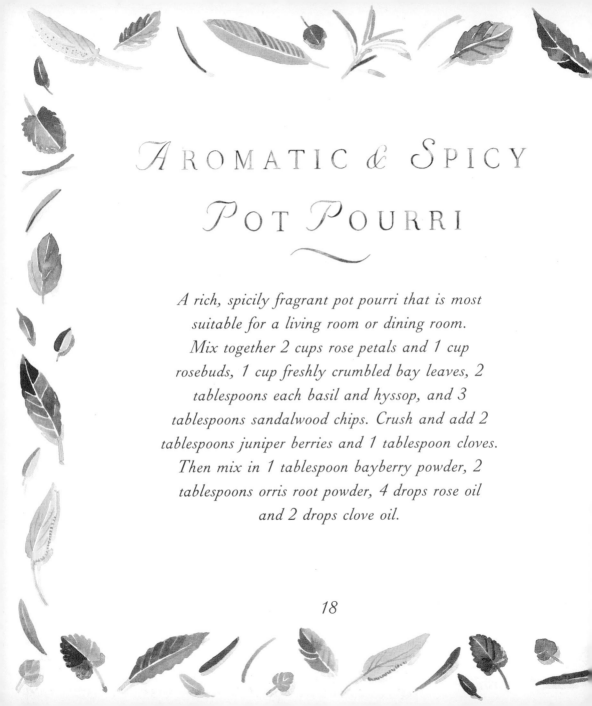

AROMATIC & SPICY
POT POURRI

A rich, spicily fragrant pot pourri that is most
suitable for a living room or dining room.
Mix together 2 cups rose petals and 1 cup
rosebuds, 1 cup freshly crumbled bay leaves, 2
tablespoons each basil and hyssop, and 3
tablespoons sandalwood chips. Crush and add 2
tablespoons juniper berries and 1 tablespoon cloves.
Then mix in 1 tablespoon bayberry powder, 2
tablespoons orris root powder, 4 drops rose oil
and 2 drops clove oil.

Sandalwood chips

rose Petals

bay leaves

basil leaves

rose buds

Cloves

hyssop

19

GOLDEN HARVEST
MEDLEY

*Poppies, wheat ears, and cornflowers have no
scent, so mix them with fragrant flowers and leaves
to make a pot pourri for harvest time.
Mix together 2 cups rose petals, 1 cup lemon balm
leaves, 1 cup poppy petals, 1 cup dried poppy seed
heads, 1 cup cornflowers, 12 wheat ears, 2
tablespoons basil, 2 tablespoons thyme, 2
tablespoons dried orange peel, crushed, and 1
tablespoon each juniper berries and blade mace,
both crushed. Add 4 tablespoons orris root powder,
3 drops each lemon balm, rose and orange
oil, and mix well.*

cornflower

blade mace

poppy seed heads

rose petals

wheat ears

orange peel

poppy petals

juniper berries

thyme

lemon balm

21

REFRESHING LAVENDER POT POURRI

*Blending lavender and herbs produces a fresh scent
ideal for the hallway, lavatory
or living room.
Mix together 2 cups lavender flowers, 1 cup
costmary, ½ cup peppermint leaves, 6 tablespoons
crushed bay leaves, and 4 tablespoons rosemary
leaves. Crush and add 2 tablespoons each juniper
and allspice berries, and then mix in 4 tablespoons
orris root powder, 4 drops lavender oil, and 2
drops each rosemary and peppermint oil.*

costmary

juniper berries

peppermint

bay leaves

rosemary

lavender

allspice
berries

23

Fresh & Reviving Pot Pourri

*A pot pourri with a fresh, clear scent, suitable for a
living room, hallway or bedroom.
Mix together 2 cups rose petals, 1 cup lavender
flowers, 1/2 cup lemon- or peppermint-scented
geranium leaves, 2 tablespoons rosemary leaves
and 1 tablespoon fragrant thyme. Crush and add 2
tablespoons allspice berries and 1 tablespoon
cloves. Add 2 tablespoons orris root powder, 5
drops rose oil and 3 drops lavender oil
and mix well.*

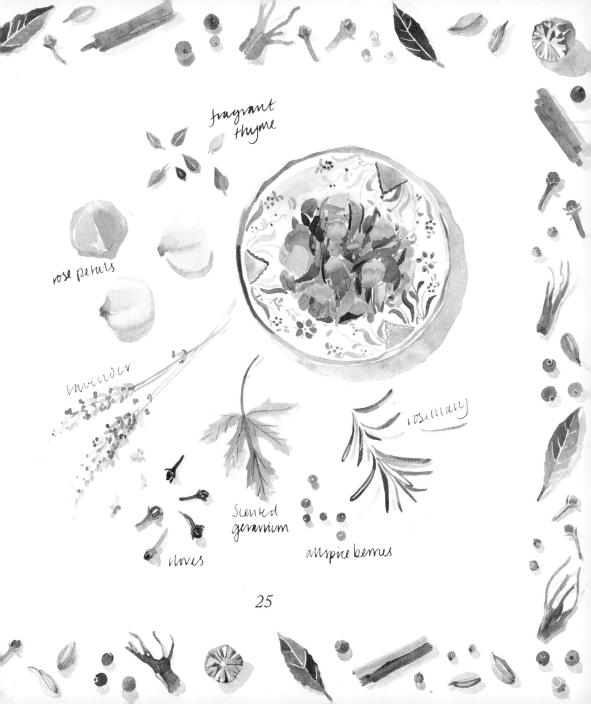

fragrant thyme

rose petals

lavender

rosemary

scented geranium

cloves

allspice berries

25

POT POURRI FOR THE KITCHEN

The tansy in this mixture will help keep away flies, besides giving a clean, savoury scent. Mix together 1 cup each tansy, southernwood, mint-scented geranium leaves and marigold flowers, and ½ cup lemon balm. Grate in 1 nutmeg, and add 4 tablespoons sandalwood powder, 2 tablespoons sanderswood raspings, and 2 tablespoons gum benzoin powder. Put in 2 drops each peppermint, cedarwood, and cypress oil, and mix well.

tansy

lemon balm

nutmeg

sanderswood raspings

scented geranium

marigold

southernwood

27

A PERFUMED SUMMER JAR

*A moist pot pourri that blends half-dried and
completely dried flowers and leaves.
Mix together 2 cups half-dried rose petals with 1
cup half-dried pinks and 1 cup half-dried jasmine
flowers. Add ½ cup fine, pure sea salt, the grated
fresh rinds of ½ orange and ½ lemon, ½ cup
dried lavender flowers, ½ cup dried marjoram, ½
cup crumbled dried bay leaves, 2 tablespoons
brandy, 2 tablespoons each cloves and allspice
berries, both crushed, and 4 tablespoons orris root
powder. Keep in a sealed jar for 3 weeks.*

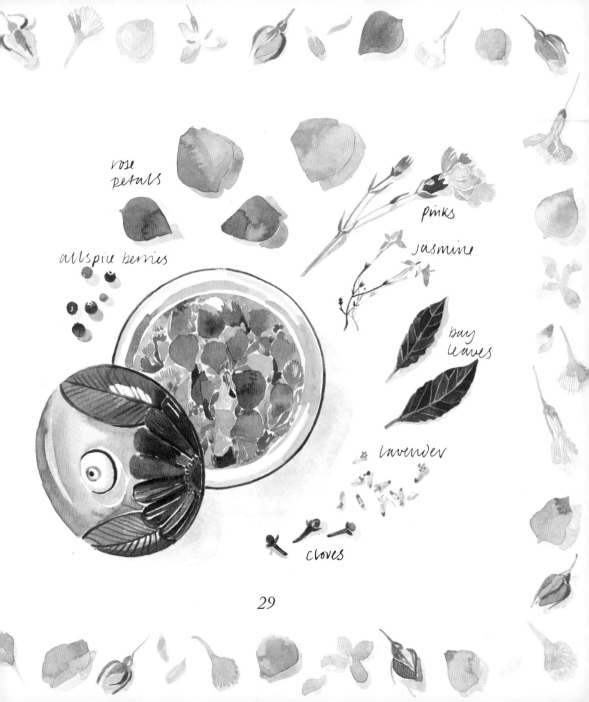

rose
petals

pinks

jasmine

allspice berries

bay
leaves

lavender

cloves

29

SLEEPY BLEND FOR THE BEDROOM

*Hops have relaxing and sleep-inducing properties,
and a pot pourri made with them can be kept in
the bedroom in an open bowl or used to fill a hop
pillow. Hops have a very strong scent and need
few extra ingredients.*

*Mix together 2 cups hops, 1 cup each woodruff,
agrimony, and southernwood, ½ cup each crushed
bay leaves and rosemary leaves, 4 tablespoons
orris root powder, 4 drops rosemary oil, and 2
drops lemon balm oil. If the mixture is to be
placed in a bowl, add dried, unscented
flowers to give some colour.*

hops

agrimony

woodruff

southernwood

rosemary

31

bay leaves

FRAGRANT CHRISTMAS BOWL POT POURRI

*Pine cones, bay leaves, and spices create a warm
rich scent for Christmas. In order to preserve a
bright, decorative colour, no orris root is included
in the ingredients. This can be added after
Christmas to preserve the scent for longer.
Roughly crumble 2 cups bay leaves and mix them
with 2 cups broken pine cones, 1 cup lemon
verbena, and 1 cup each hibiscus and paeony
petals. Add 4 tablespoons crushed cloves,
2 tablespoons bayberry powder, 2 tablespoons
sanderswood raspings plus 3 drops each clove,
lemon verbena, and sandalwood oil. Mix well.*

lemon
verbena

hibiscus
petals

pine cone

bay leaves

paeony
petals

cloves

33

DUSKY BLUE FRAGRANCE

*An unusually coloured pot pourri with a clean,
fresh scent. The proportions of the blue flowers can
be altered according to availability.
Mix together 2 cups blue hydrangea flowers,
$1/2$ cup each larkspur, borage and blue cornflowers,
1 cup lavender flowers, and $1/2$ cup crushed bay
leaves. Add 2 tablespoons each lemon thyme,
marjoram, and rosemary, 2 cinnamon sticks,
crushed, $1/2$ nutmeg, freshly grated, and 4
tablespoons orris root powder. Mix in 4 drops
lavender oil and 2 drops each rosemary
and lemon oil.*

borage

larkspur

hydrangea
flowers

lavender

bay

rosemary

cinnamon stick

thyme

cornflowers

35

St Clement's Citrus Blend

"Oranges and lemons, say the bells of St Clements." This pot pourri has the sweet, fresh scents of oranges and lemons. Use it in the living room, hall or lavatory.

Mix together 3 cups of rose petals, 1 cup lemon balm leaves, and 2 tablespoons lemon thyme. Crush and add 3 tablespoons dried orange peel and 2 tablespoons dried lemon peel, 1 tablespoon blade mace, and 1 tablespoon allspice berries. Mix in 3 tablespoons orris root powder, 2 tablespoons gum tragacanth powder, 4 drops rose oil, and 2 drops each orange and lemon oil.

rose
petals

lemon
balm

lemon
peel

lemon
thyme

orange
peel

blade mace

allspice
berries

37

A Scented
Crock of Gold

The sweet, herbal scent of this pot pourri makes it suitable for a kitchen, dining room, or living room. Mix together 2 cups marigold flowers, 1 cup yellow everlasting flowers, 1 cup chamomile flowers, ½ cup meadowsweet, and 4 tablespoons each marjoram, rue and hyssop. Add 4 tablespoons crushed, dried lemon peel, 1 nutmeg, grated, 4 drops honeysuckle oil and 2 drops lemon balm oil. Mix well.

hyssop

nutmeg

lemon peel

marjoram

everlasting flowers

marigold

meadowsweet

rue

chamomile

39

COUNTRY HOUSE POT POURRI

*The traditional method for making a
moist pot pourri.*
*In a large crock, mix as many half-dried rose
petals as you have with one third their volume of
fine, pure sea salt. Weight the mixture down and
leave it in a cool, dry place to ferment, following
the instructions given in the introduction. Break up
the finished dry mixture and measure it – for every
4 cups, add 4 tablespoons dried marjoram,
4 tablespoons crumbled dried bay leaves,
2 tablespoons ground cinnamon and
2 tablespoons gum benzoin powder.*

cinnamon

rose petals

marjoram

bay leaves

41

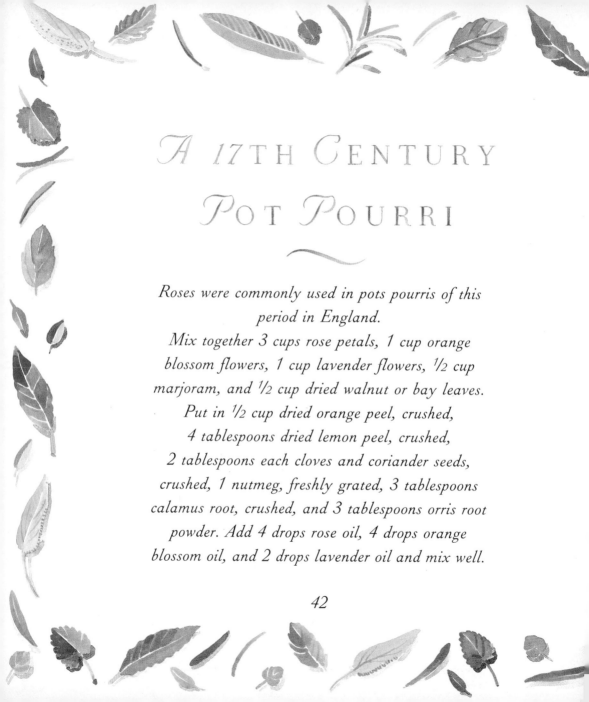

A 17TH CENTURY POT POURRI

Roses were commonly used in pots pourris of this period in England.

Mix together 3 cups rose petals, 1 cup orange blossom flowers, 1 cup lavender flowers, 1/2 cup marjoram, and 1/2 cup dried walnut or bay leaves. Put in 1/2 cup dried orange peel, crushed, 4 tablespoons dried lemon peel, crushed, 2 tablespoons each cloves and coriander seeds, crushed, 1 nutmeg, freshly grated, 3 tablespoons calamus root, crushed, and 3 tablespoons orris root powder. Add 4 drops rose oil, 4 drops orange blossom oil, and 2 drops lavender oil and mix well.

walnut leaves

cloves

nutmeg

lavender

orange blossom

orange peel

coriander seeds

marjoram

rose petals

lemon peel

43

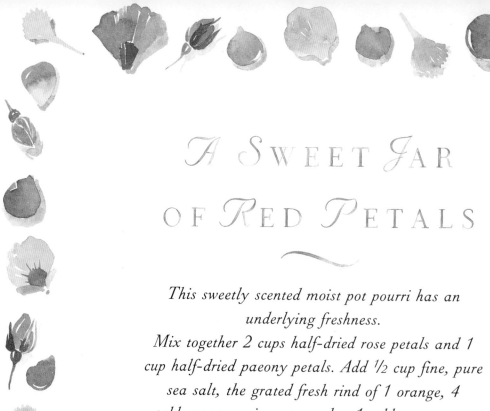

A SWEET JAR
OF RED PETALS

This sweetly scented moist pot pourri has an underlying freshness.

Mix together 2 cups half-dried rose petals and 1 cup half-dried paeony petals. Add ½ cup fine, pure sea salt, the grated fresh rind of 1 orange, 4 tablespoons orris root powder, 1 tablespoon gum benzoin powder, and 1 tablespoon crushed juniper berries. Mix well. Put the mixture into a sealed jar and leave it for 3 weeks. Shake up the pot pourri before putting it into its final container.

paeoney petals

orange rind

juniper berries

rose petals

45

An Elizabethan Pot Pourri

As spices became more readily available during the
sixteenth century, pot pourri-making increased in
popularity. Fresh scents produced from combining
spices with herbs such as lavender and peppermint
· were favoured in Elizabethan times.
Mix together 2 cups lavender flowers, 1 cup thyme,
1 cup peppermint, and 1 cup dried blue flowers for
colour. Add 2 tablespoons each cloves, coriander
seeds and caraway seeds, all crushed, 2
tablespoons crushed gum benzoin crystals, 2
tablespoons orris root powder, 4 drops lavender oil
and 2 drops peppermint oil. Mix well.

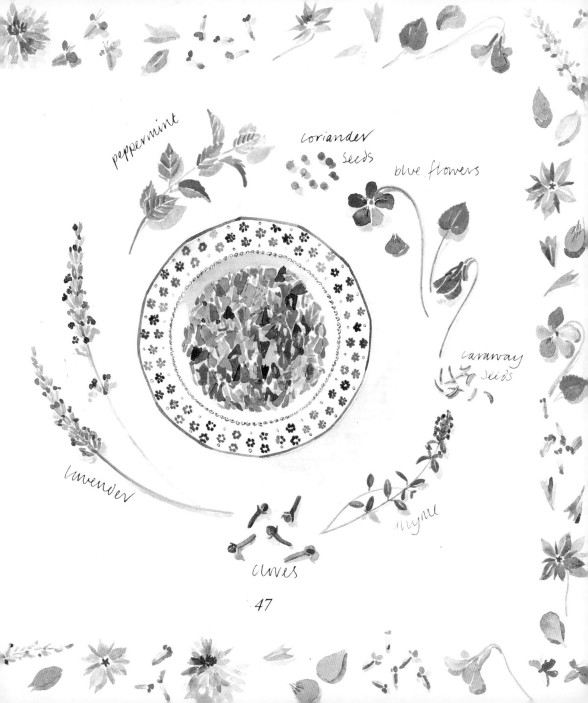

peppermint

coriander seeds

blue flowers

caraway seeds

lavender

thyme

cloves

47

Sweet Lavender Bowl

Lavender is sweet as well as refreshing and, when added to this unusual mix of herbs, spices and oils, makes a sweetly scented pot pourri that has both relaxing and refreshing qualities. Use it in the living room or bedroom.

Mix together 2 cups each lavender and lemon verbena flowers and ¹/₂ cup each marjoram and chips of sandalwood. Crush and add 4 tablespoons cloves and 2 cinnamon sticks, and then mix in 2 tablespoons each gum benzoin powder and orris root powder. Add 4 drops lemon oil and 2 drops each lemon verbena and sandalwood oil.

48

marjoram

chips
of
sandalwood

cinnamon

lavender

cloves

lemon verbena

49

SCENTED
SPRINGTIME BOWL

This is a simple pot pourri made from flowers available in the spring and early summer, plus complementing fragrant herbs. It is deliciously sweetly scented.

Mix together 3 cups lilac flowers, 1 cup wallflowers, 1/2 cup violet flowers, 1/2 cup marjoram, and 4 tablespoons rosemary. Add 4 tablespoons calamus root, crushed, 2 vanilla pods, chopped and crushed, 2 tablespoons crushed cloves, 4 tablespoons orris root powder, 2 tablespoons gum benzoin powder, 4 drops lilac oil, 2 drops violet oil and 2 drops rosemary oil.

50

wallflowers

lilac flowers

cloves

violet

marjoram

rosemary

51

POT POURRI
OF SPICED PETALS

*This moist pot pourri is made from a mixture of
spices and scented flowers.*

*In a large crock, mix together 1 cup each rose
petals, sweet-scented stocks and jasmine flowers,
all half-dried. Add 1 cup fine, pure sea salt, the
grated fresh rind of 1 lemon, 2 tablespoons ground
cinnamon and 2 tablespoons ground cloves. Mix
well and weight down, following the instructions
given in the introduction. When the mixture is
dried and pressed, add 4 tablespoons each dried
lemon thyme, hyssop, marjoram, and orris root
powder, and 2 crushed cinnamon sticks.*

52

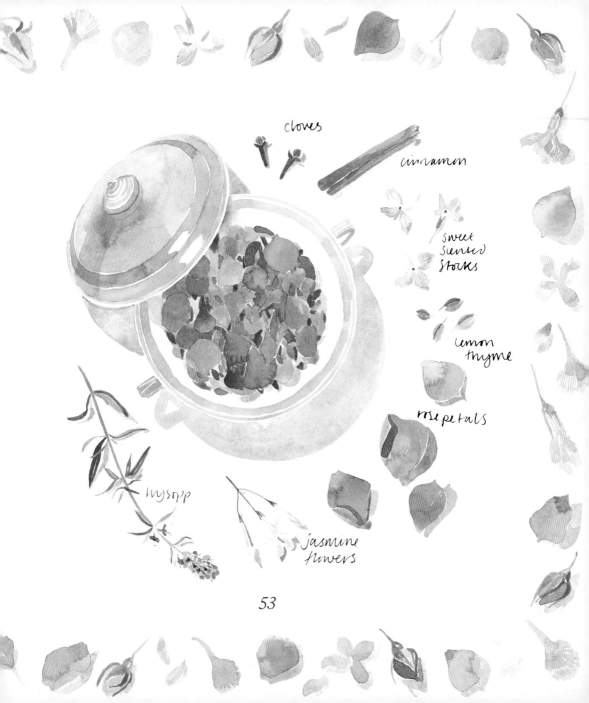

cloves

cinnamon

sweet
scented
stocks

lemon
thyme

rose petals

hyssop

jasmine
flowers

53

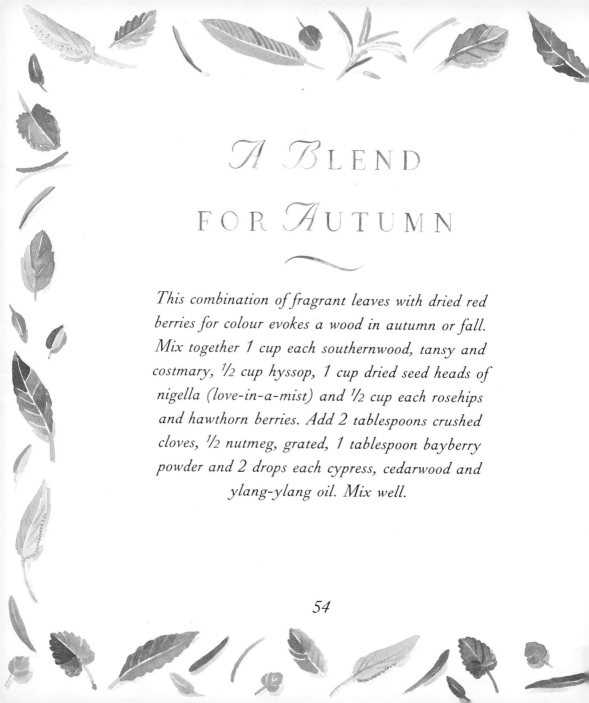

A BLEND

FOR AUTUMN

This combination of fragrant leaves with dried red berries for colour evokes a wood in autumn or fall. Mix together 1 cup each southernwood, tansy and costmary, $\frac{1}{2}$ cup hyssop, 1 cup dried seed heads of nigella (love-in-a-mist) and $\frac{1}{2}$ cup each rosehips and hawthorn berries. Add 2 tablespoons crushed cloves, $\frac{1}{2}$ nutmeg, grated, 1 tablespoon bayberry powder and 2 drops each cypress, cedarwood and ylang-ylang oil. Mix well.

cloves

hyssop

hawthorn berries

nigella seed heads

tansy

southernwood

rosehips

costmary

A POT POURRI
FOR LOVERS

The spices used in this pot pourri were once used in love potions in India and the Middle East. They give a sweetly spiced scent, making the pot pourri suitable for a bedroom.

Mix together 2 cups rosebuds and 1 cup jasmine flowers, 4 tablespoons of the raspings of sanderswood and 2 tablespoons cinnamon bark (cassia). Crush and add 2 tablespoons coriander seeds and 1 tablespoon cardamom seeds. Mix in 2 tablespoons gum benzoin powder, 4 drops rose oil and 2 drops each jasmine oil and patchouli oil.

jasmine flowers

rose buds

coriander seeds

raspings of sanderswood

cardamom

cinnamon bark

SUMMER GARDEN
BOUQUET

*Collect and dry small amounts of different flowers
throughout the summer and simply mix them.
Mix together 2 cups rose petals (or petals and
buds), 1 cup jasmine, 1 cup lavender, 1 cup paeony
petals, 1 cup carnations or pinks, 1 cup marigolds,
1/2 cup chamomile, and 1/2 cup each lemon balm,
marjoram, hyssop, thyme and peppermint, plus
any flowers purely for colour. Add 2 crushed
cinnamon sticks, 4 tablespoons crushed allspice
berries, 2 tonquin (tonka) beans, grated, 4
tablespoons orris root powder, and 2 drops each
honeysuckle, carnation, lilac and lavender oil.*

carnation

lavender

rose petals

hyssop

paeony petals

cornflowers

chamomile

marigold

lemon balm

jasmine

cinnamon

59

A GEORGIAN POT POURRI

The eighteenth century was the "golden age" of pot pourri-making in England. Each country house had its recipe, and every fragrant flower imaginable was added. This mixture has a very sweet scent. Mix together 3 cups rose petals, 1 cup lavender flowers, 1 cup clove pink flowers, 1 cup orange blossom flowers, 1 cup violet flowers, ½ cup bay leaves, crushed, and 1 cup sweet myrtle leaves. Add 2 crushed cinnamon sticks, 2 tablespoons cloves, crushed, 1 grated nutmeg, 4 drops rose oil, 2 drops carnation oil and 2 drops violet oil; mix well.

nutmeg

orange
blossom

cloves

clove pink

lavender

cinnamon
sticks

sweet
myrtle

rose petals

violets

bay leaves

61

SPRING & SUMMER MÉLANGE

All the fragrant flowers of spring and summer go into this moist pot pourri. Begin with wallflowers and lilac, and finish with the last summer roses. Half dry your petals and flowers as you harvest them. Mix them with one third their volume of fine, pure sea salt plus the grated fresh rind of 1 orange, 1 tablespoon sieved muscovado sugar, 1 tablespoon ground cloves, and 1 tablespoon ground cinnamon for every 3 cups petals. Stir into your crock throughout the summer. After the final petals have been added, weight down and complete the process as given in the introduction.

orange peel

rose petals

wallflowers

cloves

lilac

63

Gail Duff has written over thirty books and many articles on country crafts, cookery and folklore, and broadcasts regularly on radio and television.

Charlotte Wess studied illustration at Brighton Polytechnic in England. Her work has since been commissioned by publishers, magazines, design companies and advertising agencies. She has illustrated many books, including a work on the flower gardens of Gertrude Jekyll.